Commercial Con

CW01486726

THE MANAGERS GUIDE TO
UNDERSTANDING
INDEMNITY
CLAUSES

Also available in the *Commercial Contracts for Managers Series*:

- *Understanding Commercial Contract Negotiations*
- *Understanding Commonly Used Contract Terms*
- *Understanding Confidentiality Agreements*
- *Understanding Tenders*

THE MANAGERS GUIDE TO
UNDERSTANDING INDEMNITY CLAUSES

by

Frank Adoranti

Dip Law (BAB), MBA (UNE), FCIS

Solicitor and Barrister of the Supreme Court of
New South Wales

Chartered Secretary

Notary Public

LES50NS
PROFESSIONAL
PUBLISHING

First published in Great Britain 2006

LES5ONS PROFESSIONAL PUBLISHING Limited
A Division of LES5ONS (PUBLISHING) Limited
Fitzroy House
11 Chenies Street
London WC1E 7EY, United Kingdom

Email: info@fiftylessons.com

© Frank Adoranti, 2006

ISB 0-85297-760-3

Cover Designer: Insignia Graphics

Senior Editor: Jessica Perini

Printed by Loupe Solutions

PREFACE

■ ■ ■

Just because you've been signing contracts for years, it doesn't mean you have understood what you've been signing.

One of management's biggest fears is that of an employee exposing the company to the risk of potentially ruinous litigation. It is a fear with genuine foundation.

The cost of litigation is measured in the billions (indeed one estimate is that in the USA alone, the cost is in excess of $200 billion).

A company exposed to litigation suffers the following consequences:

- uncertainty;
- adverse publicity and loss of reputation; and
- expense and drain of management time.

These consequences are the natural enemies of the manager. They undermine the marketplace's perception of the company and can also have adverse effects on a company's share price. This is especially so given the post-Enron/Arthur Andersen climate of business.

During the last five years, I have devoted much time and effort to instilling a culture of litigation prevention in corporations, by the education of managers in fundamental concepts of commercial contracts.

A common question raised by managers at the conclusion of my seminars is: *What book can I read as a ready reference?* Unfortunately, I found no particular book catering to these aspects of corporate legal education. The most common problems expressed to me regarding existing books on the market were that they were:

- **too difficult to read:** the bulk of titles on the market dealing with contracts are scholarly academic works intended for the practising lawyer or law student;

- **not practical:** the less imposing and shorter "guides" are predominantly aimed at law students "cramming" or revising for examinations or oriented to consumer law issues (neighbourhood disputes, family law, wills and personal bankruptcy); and

- **not portable:** none are presented as handy reference guides specifically tailored to managers. They are usually off-putting in their size, length and/or prohibitive expense.

When discussing the concept of a manager's guide to commercial contracts, most of the comments I received from managers can be summarised in the following quotation:

> *Whilst it might not offer the depth of information on a particular topic that a textbook does, a handy guide in your briefcase accessible <u>when you need it</u> is far better than the volume/s sitting on a shelf back at your home or office.*

This provided me with the final impetus to fill the need in this area. You hold in your hands the first in a series of books catering to this requirement.

To the non-lawyer, indemnity clauses are often shrouded in mystery. The reason being that they often appear in contracts in large slabs of text using the most archaic and confusing legal terminology. They tend to appear intimidating and unintelligible to the non-lawyer, at first glance.

The purpose of this book is to provide an explanation of their function and operation as well as clear demonstrations illustrating their power. The aim is to help companies avoid the adverse publicity and drain on management resources that contract disputes and litigation present.

In addition, we will cover a number of practical tips on some of the traps and pitfalls, of which the reader should be aware, when reading indemnity clauses.

At the conclusion, the reader will be equipped and better able to critique and consider all but the most complex indemnity clauses likely to be encountered. The reader will become familiar with the language of indemnities and will develop a level of confidence to give them a working familiarity with those terms as well as being able to communicate intelligently with their legal and other advisers. As a consequence, much of the intimidation created by complex indemnity clauses, will become a thing of the past.

However, as a safeguard, we recommend that you always seek qualified legal advice in specific situations.

When dealing with the law, often, there is no single "right" answer. This series of books will help managers develop the ability to deal with particular aspects of the ambiguities of contracts. They should be of assistance to every manager dealing with commercial contracts and agreements. From sales and business development staff through to the CEO and CFO. The series caters to those in large publicly-listed organisations as well as to smaller businesses.

In writing this series, I have drawn on my 16 years of experience in the law in various countries. I have tried to cut through the mire of theory and "legalese" and distil the essence of a highly technical topic into something easily understandable and digestible for the manager in a hurry.

Where possible, I have used actual clauses, taken from commercial contracts that I have advised upon, as illustrations of many of the points made in the book.

I trust you find this series of guides as useful to read as I found them enjoyable to write.

FRANK ADORANTI

Sydney, March 2006

ACKNOWLEDGMENTS

A work which is the product of years of research and development never comes together single-handedly. I-wish to thank in particular (and in no particular order) my good friend David Crane who consistently demonstrates that he is not a "fair weather friend". To Gary Ulman, Elizabeth Crowhurst, Lindsay Powers and Michael Grider for their cheerful acceptance of the less than glamorous task of reviewing the manuscript and for providing a number of insightful and useful comments. I am grateful for your assistance. Thanks also to James-Forster, Maureen Frank and Robyn Melean for their input and critique on the warranty and indemnity insurance sections. To my editor and answerer of inane questions, Jessica Perini, thank you for your patience and guidance throughout the entire process. I must also specially commend Ross Edwards for his tireless efforts resulting in the highly readable internal layout of the books in the series and Vivien Valk for the aesthetically pleasing cover design. To my brother Gino for his valuable review comments, friendship and support, I am permanently indebted.

To my parents, for their total love, encouragement and support — which I will never be able to repay. They are my treasures. Finally, my heart belongs to my dear wife, Rosalie, the centre of my universe and award-winning mother of our beautiful (and obviously, amazingly talented) children.

ABOUT THE AUTHOR

■ ■ ■

The author has worked in the private practice of law since-1986. Since 1996 he has worked with a number of multi-national corporations both in Europe and in the Asia–Pacific region.

As an international corporate lawyer and consultant, he has reviewed thousands of significant commercial agreements and has seen, first hand, the damage that organisations suffer when proper care is not exercised in negotiating and correctly documenting contract terms. He has also conducted or managed hundreds of millions of dollars of litigation — in the USA, Europe, Australia and throughout the Asia–Pacific region — resulting from such lack of care.

He has been involved in a broad range of commercial transactions ranging from the sale of a two-and-a-half billion dollar international group of companies to simple confidentiality agreements, and much else in between. He has also assisted organisations with:

- mergers and acquisitions;
- post-merger integrations;

- litigation strategy and tactics;
- corporate restructures;
- establishment of tender and bidding processes;
- crisis management planning;
- contract management systems;
- legal audit and legal risk reviews;
- relations with external lawyers;
- planning corporate legal departments;
- compliance programs; and
- in-house training programs and seminars on contracts and other legal issues.

In addition to his qualifications as a lawyer, he has an MBA and is a Fellow of the Institute of Chartered Secretaries and Administrators. He is also a Notary Public.

TABLE OF CONTENTS

■ ■ ■

Chapter 1 **Foundation**

Chapter 2 **Why use indemnities?**

Chapter 3 **Examples**

INTRODUCTION

■ ■ ■

The aim of this book is to give managers and employees dealing with contracts a broad understanding of the nature of indemnities and their potentially devastating effects, particularly when they are not properly scrutinised and understood prior to their acceptance.

Conversely, it will become apparent that when put to use properly and intelligently, indemnity clauses can also be a very effective and powerful safeguard, or can be used as a tool to transfer or outsource risk to another party in a transaction.

It is surprising how some managers have only a rudimentary understanding of the concept of an indemnity. Indeed some of these managers have been encountering and reading indemnities for many years, often without an appreciation of their full significance.

The current climate of business is one of heightened awareness of risk and insurance issues. This stems from the recent spate of massive corporate collapses in Australia, the USA and other parts of the world.

Arising from these collapses are a number of broader issues that we can expect to become the subjects of increasing regulation such as disclosure and corporate reporting, accounting standards, directors' duties as well as broader ethical issues and general corporate governance.

Increasingly common news headlines of corporate boards having "fallen asleep at the wheel" will see tougher regulation of the activities of corporate officers and clearer definitions of their duties and obligations.

As a consequence, we can expect increasing scrutiny on the actions of directors and officers, particularly where there is a question over whether they have acted in the best interests of the shareholders.

Preventative measures and safeguards as well as ways of transferring risk to others will gain greater emphasis as directors will need to protect and shield themselves from personal liability. This is where an understanding of fundamental contract principles becomes crucial. No director wants to be exposed to personal liability because they committed their company to unduly onerous indemnities, without an appreciation of their consequences.

In addition, the insurance industry has undergone a massive change in the period post–September 11th, 2001 and post–HIH/Enron/ Arthur Andersen controversies. Premiums have risen drastically to compensate for insufficient reserves and provisioning and to deal with the increased risks that businesses currently face. Insurance regulators are now more closely monitoring insurers' liquidity obligations.

In the face of society's increasing litigiousness, the situation can only deteriorate.

Insurance companies will increasingly require that corporations implement proactive risk management programmes and strategies, with emphasis on the aim of preventing losses in the first place, rather than dealing with them once they occur.

These factors combine to make a fundamental understanding of indemnities more relevant than ever.

We will commence by going back to the very basics and explaining what indemnities are and what they are designed to achieve. Through the use of examples, we will see the differences between fair indemnity clauses and those that are unduly onerous. Through the explanations provided, you will begin to understand what factors account for these differences and how to spot them.

We'll then examine how indemnities are used to outsource or transfer risk to other parties and in which circumstances it is appropriate to do so. You will also understand what consequential loss is and why it is so powerful and hard to measure.

Finally, we will consider the interaction of indemnities and insurance and why it is unwise to have one without the other. We'll also look at the specific coverage offered by warranty and indemnity insurance and whether it might be appropriate to consider in a specific transaction.

Chapter 1

FOUNDATION

■ ■ ■

What is an indemnity?

An indemnity is a contractual commitment by a party to make good a specified loss suffered by the other party. In other words, it is an acknowledgment and promise by one party to cover the potential liability of another.

A key feature of an indemnity is that the obligation created by it can often extend *beyond* that which would otherwise be imposed on a party under the general law.

The very concept of an indemnity is to make the injured party whole again, as if the loss had not occurred, even if the person who agrees to indemnify would not otherwise have had any obligation to do so.

In contracts, the typical reasons for indemnities are:

- **Transferring or reversing liability from one party to a contract to another.** Consider a situation where **Robin** seeks to purchase a particular patented machine from the supplier, **Banks**. In the event of a claim by a third party that the use of the machine by **Robin** constituted an infringement of patent, liability would naturally fall onto **Robin**. In such an instance, a prudent buyer would seek an indemnity from the supplier (**Banks**) to protect the buyer against any such third party claims. This is an example of the reversal or transfer of liability that can be achieved with an indemnity.

- **Confirming and reinforcing existing liability.** Where a potential liability of one contracting party to the other is already the subject of a warranty, the recipient of that warranty wishes to reinforce the warranty by means of an indemnity.

  Typically, in a claim for a breach of warranty (for reasons discussed later) a claimant may not recover all of the loss incurred. The indemnity, however, will extend to cover losses that might not otherwise have been covered by a claim for damages for breach of warranty.

■ ■ ■

Language of an indemnity

At common law, indemnities are generally construed strictly according to the actual words used.

Liability will not extend beyond that which is expressly provided for in the language of the indemnity. It is not common for courts to read-in additional words when interpreting the meaning of an indemnity.

As a result, the language used in indemnities is quite cumbersome and will usually be very wide and all-inclusive in scope. Hence, wording such as the following is a common feature in the drafting of indemnity clauses:

... *damage or loss of whatsoever nature* ...

or

... *howsoever caused* ...

or

... *notwithstanding anything to the contrary contained herein* ...

Another feature of some indemnity clauses (which mercifully, seems to be appearing with decreasing frequency) is the definition of the parties to the clause:

- the party giving the indemnity (that is, the one who will have to pay the other party's bills if things go wrong) being referred to as the *indemnor*, the *indemnitor* or the *indemnifier*;

- the party having the benefit and protection of the indemnity being referred to as the *indemnee* or *indemnitee*.

Golden Rule

In "plain English", the principle to be generally applied in indemnities is:

- if we mess up, we are responsible for the direct consequences;

- if you mess up, you are responsible for the direct consequences;

- if someone under our control is to blame, we are responsible;

- if we share the blame, then we share responsibility to the extent that we are each to blame; and

- if someone other than someone under our control is to blame we are not responsible.

■ ■ ■

Difference between warranties and indemnities

A warranty is an assurance or promise in a contract. It usually relates to assurances about past or present facts in the particular transaction which is the subject of the contract.

For example, an agreement for the sale of a business might contain the following assurance or warranty:

The business has no outstanding tax liabilities.

No matter how good a party's due diligence, other "intelligence gathering" or background investigations, it cannot expect to find out *everything* about a particular transaction before entering into it. The parties will agree on price and terms based upon their actual knowledge and on the strength of the representations made by the other — typically, at the time of entering into the contract.

The purpose of the warranty is to give the recipient of that warranty the right to sue for damages, if such assurance later proves untrue or inaccurate.

The breach of a warranty gives rise to a claim for damages. Such damages, if awarded, are subject to the common law rules relating to the assessment of damages. For example, damages will be subject to the test of remoteness, the duty to mitigate the loss etc.

The ultimate effect of such common law rules is that the recipient of the warranty may recover *substantially less* than all losses connected with the breach.

A properly worded and well-worded indemnity, instead, can make the *entire* loss recoverable.

Golden Rule

An indemnity will generally allow the recovery of all loss covered by the wording of the indemnity clause, whereas an action for breach of warranty will leave it to the court to assess the extent of loss that can be recovered.

Chapter 2

WHY USE INDEMNITIES?

■ ■ ■

Purpose of an indemnity

The purpose of an indemnity clause in a contract is to protect a party from the effects of an action, non-performance, negligence or the wrongdoing of another. Essentially, it amounts to a promise to keep another party to the contract free from harm to the extent specified by the wording of the indemnity clause.

Take the example of a very simple indemnity, where there are two parties to a contract: namely **Slashem Limited** ("Slashem") and **Burnham Corp** ("Burnham").

Assume the parties are both commercial corporations and that the contract between them contains the following simple (but devastating) indemnity clause:

> **Slashem** *agrees to indemnify* **Burnham** *against the effects of fire to* **Burnham's** *premises.*

■ ■ ■

Effects of an indemnity

Sounds simple? Let's take a closer look.

In event of fire at **Burnham's** premises — **Slashem** becomes liable to pay **Burnham** the *total amount of any damage* suffered by **Burnham**.

Notice that in this example, this will apply *regardless* of how the fire started. This is because the indemnity was not qualified or limited in any way. Conceivably, therefore, it could apply even if **Burnham** had intentionally started the fire itself (putting aside criminal laws relating to arson).

For the sake of the example, let us also assume that **Burnham** owns the building it occupies.

Under the indemnity, what would **Slashem** be required to cover in the event of fire? It would be required to cover the costs of:

- replacing the building;

- replacing the contents;

- relocation during construction;

- diverting telephones and faxes and other communications;

- fitting-out the new building; and

- keeping the business functioning during the dislocation.

If we then delve further into *consequential* or *indirect loss* (topics we'll cover in more detail a little later), the prospects are virtually limitless. For example:

Burnham may have sustained a substantial and significant loss in trading profits, together with:

- loss of goodwill and reputation;

- loss of valuable (or even irreplaceable) proprietary information;

- loss of intellectual property;

- loss of data;

- years of research and development work;

- loss of lucrative existing contracts; and

- loss of prospective contracts.

■ ■ ■

Consequences of an indemnity

The consequences can be far-reaching and serious for any business not exercising due care in the indemnities it provides. Quite literally, ill-considered indemnities could lead to financial ruin.

If the business being indemnified was large enough, it would not be beyond the realms of possibility for it to cause bankruptcy to the party giving the indemnity. Consequences will be dealt with in more detail in Chapter 5 'Consequential (or indirect) loss'.

Some might be tempted to think that having insurance will be the solution to their concerns, as regards indemnities. We will see a little later why this is not necessarily the case and why insurance is not the security blanket that one might believe it to be.

■ ■ ■

Liability under an indemnity does not depend on the dollar value of the contract

Consider the following car park licence agreement. The owner of a car park (**Knott**) grants a licence to **Giltee** to park seven of its vehicles in the car park for $60 per month. **Giltee** decides that its in-house legal department does not need to review an insignificant $60 per month contract.

Buried within the agreement is a clause that reads:

The Licensee [**Giltee**] *hereby indemnifies and holds harmless the Licensor* [**Knott**, the car park owner] *in respect of and against any and all claims made by any person or persons against the Licensor for any loss damage injury or death howsoever arising within or near the Car Parking area notwithstanding any act omission or negligence of any person including but not limited to the Licensor or its agents.*

What the clause means — in plain English — is that *Giltee* takes on *all* responsibility and liability for anyone injured in the car park *for any reason*.

For example: Assume the local telephone company digs a hole in the car park and someone is unlucky enough to fall into the hole severely injuring themselves. Assume the injured person then sues **Knott** (the car park owner) seeking compensation for the injuries sustained.

Result: Pursuant to the indemnity, *Giltee* would then become liable for that injured person's loss *in its entirety*.

*The fact that **Giltee** did not cause or contribute to those injuries would have no impact on **Giltee's** obligation to pay.*

The fact that **Giltee** could exercise no control over the telephone company or its employees would also not matter. Such is the power of an indemnity.

In anyone's language, that it is one e-n-o-r-m-o-u-s risk to take on for a $60 a month deal.

| **Golden Rule** |

Note very carefully that the size or "dollar value" of a contract alone does not limit the amount of liability under an indemnity.

■ ■ ■

When should you ask for an indemnity?

Some would suggest "whenever you can".

There is no hard and fast rule that states when an indemnity is required or otherwise. It is essentially, whatever the contracting parties are able to agree upon.

An indemnity is generally desirable from a party providing goods for use by another or providing a service to another.

In considering the answer to this question, in relation to specific circumstances, it is helpful to re-state the two main reasons for using indemnity clauses and considering their applicability to such circumstances:

- Is it necessary to transfer the natural incidence of liability to another party?

  That is, if liability would naturally fall upon you in a given situation, is it necessary to transfer that liability on to another party?

- Is it necessary to confirm or reinforce the existing liability?

  That is, is it necessary to cover the gap between damages as would be assessed at common law and those that would be suffered in the event of a breach?

Consider the following case study.

Case study

Jurassic Beverages and Mammoth Enterprises

Terry Dactyl is the proprietor of a soft-drink business, **Jurassic Beverages**, that also manufactures and installs soft-drink vending machines in various locations throughout the country.

Bron Tosorus is a successful businesswoman and the proprietor of **Mammoth Enterprises**, which owns a number of desirable high pedestrian-traffic locations in the city such as train station forecourts and shopping arcades.

Terry is negotiating contract terms with **Bron** for the sale to **Mammoth** of **Jurassic's** latest product, a new drink called "Seratops".

As part of the new promotion campaign, **Terry** wishes to install his new vending machines, at **Bron's** various premises, emblazoned with his new and brightly-coloured marketing slogan "Try Seratops!".

Terry's proposal seeks an indemnity from **Mammoth** in relation to the use of the drink machines that will be installed on **Mammoth's** premises. The proposal contains the following clause:

> ***Mammoth*** *represents and warrants to* ***Jurassic*** *that it will use the Equipment for its intended purpose and agrees that it will indemnify Jurassic in respect of any loss or damage to the Equipment whether arising in*

> *the course of the intended use or otherwise.*
> ***Mammoth*** *further agrees that it will indemnify*
> ***Jurassic*** *in respect of any claim for loss,*
> *damage or injury caused to a third party user*
> *of the Equipment installed at* ***Mammoth's***
> *premises.*

Terry tells **Bron** that if the machines are vandalised and as a result, soft-drink leaks on to the floor and a shopper or train passenger slips, that is her problem. He also says that if a customer loses money due to vandalism, **Bron** should have to compensate the customer. He says that he is looking to **Mammoth** to "see him right" if the product is stolen and/or the vending machines are attacked.

Bron's response to **Terry's** initial proposal is set-out below:

Dear **Terry***,*

The terms of your document are unacceptable in that we do not wish to:

1. *Indemnify you in respect of your drink machines.*

   To the contrary, we will require you to indemnify us in relation thereto.

As both the product and machines are yours, a reasonable starting point is for prima facie liability to rest with you, the manufacturer, if the product or machines cause injury, death, loss or damage.

2. *Insure or maintain the machines.*

3. *Be liable for any loss or damage. These are your machines, which you own and have the responsibility to maintain. You must, therefore, warrant to us their suitability and safety. If there is an injury or loss as a result of the machine's use in the ordinary course, it is your responsibility.*

4. *In addition, you give no warranty of safety in relation to the products being dispensed though the machines.*

We propose the following clauses for use in the supply agreement:

Jurassic warrants the safety of the Products and/or the Equipment and shall bear the risk of any loss or damage (except for loss resulting from the negligence or wilful act of Mammoth) and shall fully maintain and insure the same against all risks. Mammoth shall provide a power connection (and shall not be liable for any loss, damage, injury or *death caused by any failure or irregularity thereof) at its own cost as necessary for the operation of the Equipment. **Mammoth** agrees to use the Equipment for its intended purpose.*

AND

***Jurassic** shall indemnify **Mammoth** in respect of any claim made by or against it for loss, damage, expense, cost, injury or loss of life occurring as a result of or arising from the use of the Product/s and/or Equipment by its employees, customers, invitees or any other person. Provided that any liability of **Jurassic** shall be reduced to the extent that such loss, damage or injury was caused by or contributed to by the negligence of **Mammoth**. In the event of any claim arising under this clause the parties shall work together and shall cooperate with each other to properly establish the cause of such loss or injury.*

As discussed, we have drafted the clauses with a view to achieving balance in the respective duties of the parties to the transaction.

Sincerely,
Bron.

In what circumstances might **Terry's** request have been a valid one?

Assume the agreement reached between them provided that **Bron** was to maintain the machines and was to be paid in return for doing so. If she were to refuse or fail to comply with the agreement and further refused **Terry** access to the machines, a request for an indemnity on **Terry's** part might then start to seem justified.

In such an event, Bron's action may become an intervening cause; in a similar way to that if she were to tamper with the product or machine, thereby making it unsafe.

Many would consider the position **Bron** adopted in her letter to be reasonable.

She is a passive player in the scenario. Anything that could go wrong with either the soft-drink product or the machine, are essentially **Terry's** responsibility and such matters are under his effective control.

Bron has no way of ascertaining whether the drink contained within the sealed cans is safe to consume. She has no way of knowing whether the drink machines have been maintained correctly and are safe to use.

She is relying upon the manufacturer and installer to assure her of these matters. Otherwise, she has no desire to place any object upon her property that may likely give rise to a loss or injury being occasioned to persons upon her premises.

As an aside, note that certain jurisdictions have consumer and product safety laws that cannot be excluded contractually. Depending upon the jurisdiction, some warranties (particularly consumer and product safety ones) are implied by law and cannot be excluded by a cleverly worded clause in a contract.

Some parties, such as investment banks, for example, tend to adopt a blanket policy of never giving indemnities.

You should consult your lawyer when determining:

- whether to use an indemnity clause in a particular transaction or situation;

- which party will be required to give it; and

- in what terms it should be given.

Chapter 3

EXAMPLES

███

A "fair" and balanced indemnity clause

When using the word "fair" in the heading above, it should be placed in its correct context. A "fair" indemnity clause does not seek to avoid a party's responsibility or liability for its actions. It merely seeks to limit the extent of liability to that which may be *directly* attributable to any negligence or wrongdoing.

Example

We will dissect a sample indemnity clause and examine the functions of its various components individually, to see how they operate. For the purposes of the example, let us assume the situation is a contract for the performance of services by a

Contractor to a Principal, both of which are corporations. Also assume the context of a transaction where the parties to the contract are to have rights and responsibilities shared equally.

FIGURE 1: DISSECTION OF A FAIR AND EVENLY BALANCED INDEMNITY CLAUSE

The Contractor shall indemnify the Principal against *(a) Loss or damage to any property; and* *(b) Claims by the Principal or claims by any person against the Principal in respect of personal injury, or death.*	This is the operative part of the indemnity. It specifies the nature of the consequences indemnified against: (a) loss to property; (b) personal injury or death.
arising out of or as a consequence of the Contractor's negligence in carrying out the Services.	This operates to limit the indemnity only to matters arising out of or as a consequence of negligence in carrying out the services. Note the two restrictions: firstly to negligence; secondly, to the services.
The Contractor's liability to indemnify the Principal shall be reduced to the extent that such loss, damage, injury or death was caused or contributed to by the act, omission, direction or negligence of the Principal, its servants, agents or any third party over which the Contractor does not have direct control.	This wording further limits liability under the indemnity in the proportion that fault lies either with the Principal (or any person over which the Principal has authority) or anyone else not under the control of the Contractor.

FIGURE 1 — *continued*

This clause shall not extend to include any consequential loss, damage, injury or death.	These are the words explicitly excluding any indirect or consequential damages. However, they would not exclude loss of profits.

An exception to the use of a "fair" indemnity clause

A "fair" and balanced indemnity clause would not be appropriate in a situation where, for example, a customer had a critical need for a particular service or product and a supplier had absolutely and unconditionally guaranteed to deliver that service or product "no excuses, no matter what" (and had priced such product or service as a mission-critical deliverable). In such a case, the customer would be paying a premium price for the product or service to be provided regardless of external circumstances, and would wish to be so protected by a so-called "unfair" indemnity clause.

Relief of obligations during certain "defined" events

In most "conventional" business transactions, a party may make specific allowances relieving the other party from performing its obligations under the contract during certain *defined* events outside the control of that party. This is referred to as *force majeure*. In many jurisdictions, there is no law that defines what constitutes a *force majeure* event. It will usually depend upon what the parties can negotiate and agree upon.

Given the differences in the way *force majeure* is recognised in different jurisdictions, it is prudent practice to use the *force majeure* concept as a specifically defined term in a contract. Such a clause should fully set-out as a minimum:

- A definition of the events which may be considered *force majeure* events.

- How and when notification to the other party of such event occurring should take place. Ideally, the clause can be made conditional upon the procedure being followed.

- The extent of suspension of the obligation during a *force majeure* event.

Depending on the circumstances of a particular transaction and how the parties view them, *force majeure* events can sometimes include strikes and industrial disputes (although this can sometimes be a hotly contested point), wars, riots, acts of God, etc.

■ ■ ■

An "unfair" indemnity clause

Let us now examine the other side of the coin and understand which components of an indemnity clause can cause it to be unfairly balanced in favour of one party.

The following clause creates a potential liability that is unfairly (again, assuming a "conventional" business transaction as described earlier) skewed in favour of the Principal.

That is to say, the Contractor in the following example bears all of the liability, even if the Principal has acted negligently.

There are no mechanisms limiting or reducing the Contractor's liability for losses or damages not caused by the Contractor's actions.

In rare instances, this approach may be entirely justified, but is certainly not the norm for ordinary commercial transactions.

FIGURE 2: DISSECTION OF AN UNFAIR AND UNEVENLY BALANCED INDEMNITY CLAUSE

The Contractor will be liable and hereby indemnifies the Principal for any and all loss or damage, personal injury or death	The operative part of the indemnity. Specifying the nature of the consequences indemnified against: loss and damage, personal injury and death no matter how it is caused.
(including any indirect or consequential losses damages injury or death) of whatsoever nature or kind and howsoever caused	This opens the door to consequential loss. There is an explicit reference covering loss or damage etc of whatsoever nature. This is virtually limitless.
suffered by the Principal, its officers, servants or agents, or anyone claiming through or against the Principal	The Principal can claim if it suffers the loss or damage or any of its sub-contractors. Here's the crunch: if anyone sues or claims against the Principal, the indemnity operates to protect the Principal. In other words, the Contractor will almost always be responsible.
notwithstanding the negligence of any party including the Principal.	This is the "killer". You must indemnify even if the Principal's negligence caused the loss. The trigger for the indemnity is the Principal's loss. Notice, there is no restriction for the loss arising "out of the services" being supplied.

Chapter 4

PITFALLS

■ ■ ■

Two common traps with indemnities

Indemnity clauses are often the source of much attention and angst for organisations and individuals alike. This is because of the far-reaching (and enormously costly) effects that poorly worded indemnity clauses can have on a company's "bottom line".

A properly worded indemnity clause, on the other hand, can prevent claims occurring outside the control or conduct of the person providing the indemnity.

The purpose of an indemnity clause is to protect a party from the effects of non-performance, negligence or the wrongdoing of another. Sometimes though, some unscrupulous players may see it as a way of "trapping" another party into liability and responsibility for the wrongdoing of the other.

Two common traps with indemnity clauses are the following:

1) **Where there is no exception for the negligence of the other party.**

   Some organisations *unknowingly* accept indemnity clauses making them responsible for the negligent acts of the other party!

   It is important when dealing with indemnities that *specific exception* is made for the situation where the negligence of others causes the damage or loss.

2) **Where one party agrees to accept responsibility for the acts of "invitees" or other 3rd parties over which they do not exercise control.**

   This is a significant point. In many jurisdictions, an invitee can extend to include a customer lawfully on the premises. An invitee does not necessarily have to be "invited" onto the premises. For example, a customer in a shop is lawfully on the premises if that person simply walks in.

There is always a great degree of risk whenever you accept responsibility for the acts of persons not under your direct control (for example, persons who are not either your employees or sub-contractors).

Golden Rule

Given their complexity and significance, it is important that any indemnity clause be checked before use or acceptance in any particular circumstance or contract.

It is equally dangerous to use generic or "cut-and-paste" clauses without first checking with a qualified legal adviser.

■ ■ ■

Reasons why indemnity clauses may generally be deficient

1) **Liability extends well beyond the terms of the contract or even for negligence alone.**

An indemnity clause provides as follows:

Example: *Lyon indemnifies* **Cheaton** *for any loss or damage that may be sustained or suffered by* **Cheaton**.

Problem: Under this clause, the trigger for the obligation to indemnify is not restricted to either a breach of the terms of the contract or even further restricted to negligence alone.

Under this clause, there is *no* restriction *whatsoever* on the circumstances in which liability is created. Once **Cheaton** suffers any loss for any reason (no matter how unconnected to any action of **Lyon**'s), **Lyon**'s liability to indemnify **Cheaton** is created.

Solution: You should seek to limit liability under an indemnity to keep it within the contract terms by using words such as:

... acts or omissions in connection with or arising out of the terms of the contract between the parties.

OR

To restrict liability even further to negligent acts or omissions only

You should seek to limit liability under an indemnity only for negligent acts or omissions under the contract, using wording such as:

... negligent acts or omissions in connection with or arising out of the terms of the contract between the parties.

Amended Clause:

The added words have been underlined.

Lyon indemnifies Cheaton for any loss or damage that may be sustained or suffered by Cheaton <u>as a result of any act or omission by</u> Lyon <u>in connection with or directly arising out of the terms of the contract between the parties</u>.

OR

Lyon indemnifies Cheaton for any loss or damage that may be sustained or suffered by Cheaton <u>as a result of any negligent act or omission by</u> Lyon <u>in connection with or directly arising out of the terms of the contract between the parties</u>.

2) **There is no exception for the negligent acts or omissions of third parties not under the direct control of the party giving the indemnity.**

Consider the following clause.

Example: *Lyon indemnifies* **Cheaton** *for any loss or damage that may be sustained or suffered by* **Cheaton** *as a result of any negligent act or omission of any person.*

Problem: Why would you want to take responsibility for someone else's negligence? Particularly, if it is someone over whom you cannot exercise any degree of control such as an employee or a contractor.

Solution: **Amended Clause:**

The added words have been underlined.

Lyon indemnifies **Cheaton** *for any loss or damage that may be sustained or suffered by* **Cheaton** *as a result of any negligent act or omission of any person* under the direct control of **Lyon** including his employees, agents and contractors.

3) **There is no exception for the negligence, acts or omissions of the other party to the contract.**

Consider the following clause.

Example: *Lyon indemnifies* **Cheaton** *for any loss or damage that may be sustained or suffered by* **Cheaton** *as a result of any negligent act or omission of any person under the direct control of* **Lyon** *including his employees, agents and contractors, notwithstanding any negligence of* **Cheaton**.

Problem: In this instance, **Lyon** would be liable even though **Cheaton's** loss may have been caused by its own negligence.

Why would you want to be liable for the negligence of the other party (in the absence of a specific reason)?

Note that under the above clause, such liability could even extend to include any *intentional* and negligent act.

In a practical context, such a contractual arrangement could easily become entirely unworkable.

Solution: Either replace the word *notwith-standing* with *excepting.*

Or delete the words *notwithstanding any negligence of* **Cheaton***.*

4) **There is no reduction in liability *to the extent* of negligence.**

Example: Consider the following indemnity clause in a contract for the lease of a warehouse that provides:

The **Tenant** *shall indemnify the* **Landlord** *against all damages, losses, actions, claims and demands for which the* **Landlord** *shall or may become liable arising from:*

(a) the overflow or leakage of water in the premises, caused or contributed to by any act or omission on the part of the **Tenant***;*

(b) the loss, damage or injury from any cause whatsoever to any person caused or contributed to by the use of the premises by the **Tenant** *or any other person claiming through the* **Tenant***;*

(c) *the loss, damage or injury from any cause whatsoever to any property within or outside the premises occasioned or contributed to by any act, omission, neglect or default of the **Tenant** or any other person claiming through the **Tenant**.*

Problem: It can sometimes happen that more than one party alone can be blamed for causing a particular loss. In such cases, the apportionment of responsibility becomes relevant in determining the amount of the loss payable by each of them. Assume in this case that the Tenant was 5% to blame for the cause of the loss and that another party (other than the landlord) was 95% to blame.

Under the above clause, the mere fact of *any* contribution to the loss by the Tenant would trigger the operation of the indemnity against the Tenant.

In other words, the Tenant would be liable for 100% of the loss even if that person were only 5% to blame.

Solution: By amending sub-clauses a), b) and c), as shown below, the Tenant's liability to the Landlord will be limited *to the extent* of the Tenant's contribution to the event causing the loss.

Therefore, if the Tenant is only 5% responsible for the loss, that person will be liable to pay for only 5% of the damage. Without such amendments, a slight contribution to the loss would trigger the Tenant having to give *total coverage* to the Landlord under the indemnity.

Amended Clause:

The added words have been underlined. One word is ~~deleted~~.

The change to the words is minor, however, the effect of such change could be major.

The **Tenant** *shall indemnify the* **Landlord** *against all damages, losses, actions, claims and demands for which the* **Landlord** *shall or may become liable arising from:*

(a) the overflow or leakage of water in the premises ~~or~~ _to the extent_ caused or contributed to by any act or omission on the part of the Tenant;

(b) the loss, damage or injury from any cause whatsoever to any person _to the extent_ caused or contributed to by the use of the premises by the Tenant or any other person claiming through the Tenant;

(c) the loss, damage or injury from any cause whatsoever to any property within or outside the premises _to the extent_ occasioned or contributed to by any act, omission, neglect or default of the Tenant or any other person claiming through the Tenant.

Golden Rule

In indemnities, care must be taken to address the situation where two or more parties may potentially be responsible for a loss.

Liability should be apportioned _to the extent_ of each party's responsibility.

5) **There is no specific and express exclusion for consequential or indirect loss or damage.**

Solution: You must limit your liability only to direct loss and damage by adding specific words to that effect to the end of an indemnity clause. Generally, either of the following phrases will suffice:

This shall not extend to include any consequential loss, damage or injury.

Or

Expressly excluding any consequential or indirect loss, damage or injury.

Why bet your whole company on an unknown and variable such as consequential loss? Additional detail on consequential loss follows in the next chapter.

Chapter 5

CONSEQUENTIAL (OR INDIRECT) LOSS

■ ■ ■

Rationale

Normal loss is the loss suffered as a *direct* result of a breach or action. Whereas, consequential loss is the loss suffered because of *circumstances peculiar to a particular person or entity.*

To reiterate, a "fair" indemnity clause does not seek to avoid a party's responsibility or liability for its actions. It merely seeks to limit the extent of liability to that which may be *directly* attributable to any negligence or wrongdoing.

The absence of a consequential loss provision, allows the company giving the indemnity to accurately identify and measure the extent and nature of potential losses. This allows a company to more accurately quantify and manage its risk accordingly.

It can be argued that consequential loss clauses are not normal or reasonable commercial terms.

Consequential losses, by their nature, are uncertain and difficult to quantify. They involve the acceptance of responsibility for risks that are not within the ordinary knowledge of the party giving the indemnity. In addition, they can, in some circumstances, even extend to include the losses of persons who are not parties to the agreement!

It can, therefore, be argued that a clause allowing consequential damages to be claimed *would unfairly broaden and extend liability beyond the normal commercial realm.*

As with all things in the law, the choices are often not restricted to either black or white. Compromise is an essential feature of successful negotiations over commercial contracts.

The choice confronting a party to a commercial contract might often be either to accept a consequential loss clause or not.

Alternatively, where a party has specific concerns relating to a *particular* event of consequential loss, it may be possible for the parties to direct their minds to dealing specifically and only with such an event, to attempt to find a mutually acceptable solution to the problem.

However, there may be situations in which the acceptance of consequential loss provisions is unavoidable.

In some instances, one may be compelled — by commercial considerations — to accept a consequential loss clause. For example, an airline caterer would find it very difficult in arguing against the inclusion of such a clause in its agreement with an airline.

In such an instance, one way of managing such an exposure might be acceptance of the clause with a ceiling or "cap" on the maximum liability.

Prudence might also necessitate having proper insurance coverage as a back-up to such a consequential loss indemnity provision.

Case study: the potential impact of consequential loss clauses

Food Services Contractor (Sal Monella)

Background

Food services contractor Sal Monella is negotiating to operate in-store cafeterias for a major national department store (whose shares are publicly traded on the stock exchange).

The national department store wishes to include a provision in the contract whereby Sal is responsible for and indemnifies the store against any consequential loss.

What issues does Sal face?

Consider a worst-case scenario of food poisoning. Of course, Sal would be liable for the *direct* effects upon the unfortunate individuals who consumed the bad food and fell ill. Conceivably, this could include medical bills, lost time from work etc. Sal accepts this as a normal risk inherent in his core business of supplying food. Sal's experience in managing and controlling such risks is an integral part of the service and of the expertise that it provides to his customers.

It is only natural for the store to demand an indemnity from Sal to cover it against the effects of any such events.

However, consequential loss goes well beyond this point.

Additional impact of consequential loss

Given the location of the cafeterias and the manner in which they are operated, it is reasonable to assume that the public would associate them with the store owner, not Sal. Notwithstanding any signage that might indicate that the cafeteria is being operated by Sal, the public would be placing their trust in the store owner in selecting a suitable and competent operator for their premises.

Accordingly, a major food poisoning instance, could adversely impact the store owner in two forms:

(1) Loss of retail store revenue due to customers being "scared-off" by a food poisoning incident; and

(2) Loss of reputation and the tarnishing of the department store brand in the eyes of the consuming public. The bigger the brand, the higher the potential for loss.

In addition, there are other significant flow-on effects. Notably, an adverse impact upon the share price of the store owner, attributable to such an incident. Imagine (hypothetically, for the purpose of this exercise) if the store we were dealing with was as large and high profile as say Harrods or David Jones. Such losses could easily bankrupt Sal.

Chapter 6

OUTSOURCING RISK

■ ■ ■

Rationale

As companies become more risk-aware and risk-averse, the trend to increase the outsourcing of risk to a contractor will continue. Often, in the push to do so, inequities arise in the fair apportionment of risk.

Increasingly, companies conducting tenders for the provision of goods and/or services are asking tenderers to commit to unduly onerous contract terms in their bid documents. There is increasing pressure on tenderers not to submit tenders that are "non-compliant".

"Non-compliant" referring to the number of objections or issues raised in relation to the terms of a contract which is usually attached to and forms part of tender documentation.

The organisation conducting the tender may typically apply pressure to a prospective tenderer to accept and agree to the terms of the tender documents without qualification or condition. Such pressure could take the form of hints, insinuations or explicit statements to the effect that a tender bid's chances of success will decrease with the higher number of non-compliances.

This puts a great deal of pressure on a tenderer to fall into the trap of the mentality that:

> *Other companies will agree to these clauses, therefore, in order to be competitive, we must do the same.*

Succumbing to that temptation can sometimes lead to ruin.

Conversely, boundless savings can result to the company that has successfully outsourced such liability. However, in any such one-sided arrangement, the relationship may tend to be short-lived.

Case study: outsourcing risk by using indemnities

Spit and Polish Contract Cleaning Services

Background

Charles Sheene, the principal of Spit and Polish, a contract cleaning service is negotiating a contract to clean a number of shopping centres nationwide. The party with which it is negotiating is called Fleecem, a large agency specialising in shopping centre management (we will refer to them as "the Managers").

The Managers represent Shop Till You Drop which owns a number of large shopping centres nationwide (we will refer to them as "the Owner").

The contract cleaning industry is typically characterised as having low profit margins and high competition. The barriers to entry into the industry are relatively low.

In shopping centres in particular, the incidence of "slip-and-fall" cases is ever-increasing. Generally, a large volume of such cases are uneconomical to fight in court and all parties thus seek to dispose of them quickly and commercially. Often, the cleaning contractor is the easiest party to blame as it is the cleaner's contractual responsibility to ensure that floors are free of substances and conditions that would give rise to customers falling and injuring themselves.

The Managers have proposed the following scenario to Mr Sheene and have asked Mr Sheene to agree to it in order to win the contract. The proposal devised by the Managers is an elegantly simple one, as follows:

> *Mr Sheene would take on all of the insurance and liability obligations of the Owner and the Managers of the shopping centre and would indemnify the centre Owner and the Managers against all liability for any claims. Of course, Mr Sheene could factor into his quotation the additional insurance costs. The concept being that one party indemnifies all the others, thereby eliminating duplication of separate insurance policies for Mr Sheene, the Owners and the Managers with just one policy of insurance in the name of Mr Sheene.*

Rationale for the proposal put forward by the Shopping Centre Managers

- The proposal will create substantial savings on the cost of insurance.

- The cleaning contractor is generally responsible for seven out of 10 "slip and fall" cases occurring in shopping centres.

- The proposal will create significant savings on legal fees, since you eliminate the cost of three separate legal teams (one each for the shopping centre Owner, Managers and cleaning contractor) engaged in three separate defences.

- It should reduce the number of contested claims (the so-called "cut-throat" defence, where each defendant hopes to escape liability by implicating the other).

- It reduces the burden and cost of administration.

Note that these savings and benefits accrue only to the shopping centre Owner and Managers.

What issues does Mr Sheene face?

Under the Managers' proposal, the Owner and Manager *completely* outsource their liability to Mr Sheene.

This extends to include matters totally unconnected with the cleaning services that Mr Sheene provides. The result is that Mr Sheene takes on a liability profile totally disproportionate with the scope of the cleaning services to be provided.

What liabilities are being transferred to Mr Sheene?

(1) By agreeing to cover the Owner's risk, Mr Sheene would, in effect, become responsible and liable for the *structure* and *maintenance* of the building;

(2) Consider the liability of Mr Sheene in the following instances, under the Managers' proposal:

- If there was a structural failure in the shopping centre (and assuming such failure is totally unconnected with the cleaning services) and such failure caused injury or death to persons therein — Mr Sheene <u>would be liable</u>.

- If a robbery took place in the shopping centre and persons were injured or killed (again, even if unconnected with the provision of the services) — Mr Sheene <u>would be liable</u>.

- In the event of fire (again, even assuming it was entirely unconnected with the provision of the cleaning services) and such fire caused damage or resulted in death or injury — Mr Sheene <u>would be liable</u>.

In the situations listed above, it is clearly inappropriate and unconscionable for such liability — so far removed from the nature of the cleaning services being provided — to fall upon the cleaning contractor.

Notice the power and potential effects of a carefully worded indemnity clause.

Chapter 7

INSURANCE ISSUES

∎ ∎ ∎

Terminology

Firstly, we shall define some basic terminology to facilitate an understanding of the material presented in this chapter.

Note that the two parties in a policy of insurance are typically the *insurer* (the insurance company) and the *insured* (the person or entity covered by the policy).

Disclosure letter

In an agreement for a sale of business or company, the agreements often contemplate that the vendors will disclose to the purchaser certain matters that would (or could) otherwise give rise to a claim under the warranties. The effect of this disclosure will be that the purchaser will be unable to use any of the disclosed matters as the basis for a claim under the warranties. The disclosure letter is usually the subject of intense negotiations.

Due diligence

This is the process of investigation and detailed review of all aspects of a company or business being acquired. Its culmination produces a report high-lighting any potential liability or issues which may affect or be of interest to a purchaser.

It is usually a multi-faceted approach consisting of at least the following components:

- legal due diligence;

- tax due diligence;

- accounting due diligence; and

- commercial due diligence.

Of course, the more complex the transaction, the more involved a due diligence can be.

Escrow

Funds held in escrow are withheld from their ultimate beneficiary (typically by the lawyer for the other party — in a trust account) pending the fulfilment of specified events or conditions.

Excess

An excess represents the portion of the loss that must be borne by the insured. For example, in a motor vehicle insurance policy the insured may be responsible for the first $1000 of loss occurring before the insurer is required to pay out under the policy.

The excess can sometimes be increased to obtain a reduction in the premium. The reason for an excess is usually an underwriting measure or to "filter" out small claims.

Note with caution, the terms "excess" and "deductible" are often used interchangeably. It is *not*, in fact, correct to do so.

An excess is said to sit below the sum insured. Therefore, if you have $10 million insurance cover with a $1 million excess, the insured is liable for the first $1 million and the insurer is then liable for up to $10 million *over and above that first $1 million.*

On the other hand, if you have $10 million insurance cover with a $1 million deductible, the insured is liable for the first $1 million and the insurer is then liable for up to $9 million above that first $1 million. Note that the difference is that the deductible erodes or reduces the insurer's liability by the amount of such deductible.

Proposal form

This contains all of the information upon which an insurer bases its decision to insure, and if so, upon what terms. You are required to exercise the utmost good faith when completing a proposal and ensure that you disclose *all* relevant facts and circumstances to the insurer. If you do not do so, in the event of a claim, an insurer may become entitled to reduce or to even possibly avoid *any* payment altogether under the policy.

Note that your duty of disclosure is not satisfied just by fully completing the proposal form. If the form is silent on a material fact of which you are aware, you must disclose such fact or facts fully to the insurer.

Subrogation

An insurer that has paid a loss under a policy is entitled to "step into the shoes" of the insured and have all the rights that belong to the insured against any third party in relation to the loss covered. Most typical policy wording will allow an insurer to take action in the insured's name before an indemnity payment is even made.

For example, if you make a claim against your motor vehicle policy for damage caused to your vehicle by another party, you subrogate your right of claim against the responsible party to the insurer.

A waiver of subrogation occurs when you give another party — against which an insurer may have had a right of recovery — a contractual release from any recovery against that party.

■ ■ ■

Can I "breathe easy" knowing I have an indemnity to protect me?

The simple answer is "No".

An indemnity on its own — no matter how cleverly worded — may not be sufficient to protect you.

An indemnity is only as good as the financial strength and stability of the party providing it.

For example, in a "high stakes" multi-million dollar contract:

- an indemnity from General Motors is probably a safe bet;

- an indemnity from Heretoday-Gonetomorrow Pty Limited may not be.

If a party providing an indemnity is of questionable financial strength, the indemnity could potentially be worthless. Indeed some unscrupulous companies voluntarily give some of the most generous and onerous indemnities, knowing full well that they may not necessarily be around long enough to have to pay out on them.

Accordingly, it pays to beware of any party volunteering too cheerfully to give you the most onerous (upon them) and one-sided indemnity clause. Chances are, they might know something you don't about their own future.

Remember the old saying about things appearing to be *too* good to be true.

> ## *Golden Rule*
>
> Note that the value and protection offered
> by an indemnity completely and totally
> depends upon the *future financial strength
> and stability of the party giving it.*

One solution to such a dilemma, could be Warranty
and Indemnity insurance (see page 69).

■ ■ ■

Beware of clauses purporting to restrict your insurer

Beware of indemnity clauses that attempt to restrict
or otherwise limit the ability of your insurance
company to either conduct a defence of any claim
or to claim contribution from another party found
to be full or partly responsible for any loss.

Some of the limits or restrictions generally
include the following scenarios:

● Granting the right to the other contracting party to
  appoint lawyers to defend a claim on your behalf.
  Typically, if you make a claim under your insurance

policy, your insurer will appoint its own lawyers to defend the claim in your name. Insurers will not generally agree to any provision which permits anyone else to appoint lawyers to defend claims on its behalf.

- A proposal that might exclude the right of your insurer to claim contribution from another party or from their insurers. This is called a waiver of subrogation. In this event you are being called upon to waive rights that you have granted to your insurer under your contract of insurance.

- A provision which requires you or your insurer to give notice to a party with whom you are contracting direct notice of alterations to or cancellation of your insurance policies.

As a general rule, your agreement to any of the above scenarios — or ones similar in nature and effect — is not recommended.

Attempting to limit your insurer's rights — in the absence of your insurer's express written consent to do so — could lead to a situation where your insurance company may be sufficiently prejudiced by your actions, that it may even be entitled to avoid covering you under the policy.

If you are in any doubt about the impact of an indemnity clause upon your insurance coverage, you should consult your insurance broker or insurance company *prior to acceptance of the clause.*

■ ■ ■

Won't the loss be covered by insurance?

Some may be tempted to say, *I do not have to concern myself about the form of an indemnity that I give, as I have insurance to cover such events.* This is not always the case.

Common features of insurance policies are:

- an excess — below which, coverage will not apply;

- an upper limit or ceiling — above which, coverage will not apply; and

- specific and defined *exclusions* from any coverage.

An insurer may find an exclusion or other breach of the policy and could possibly avoid having to provide coverage under the policy.

Assuming that coverage would apply, a loss incurred by a business of a considerable size, could easily exceed the limit of the insurance policy. That amount in excess of the policy's coverage would fall to be paid by the party giving the indemnity. To add further insult to injury, the premium for the next year's insurance coverage could increase exponentially. In extreme cases, an insurer could even decline to offer further future coverage.

In an instance where coverage did not extend or apply, the liability to pay would then fall *entirely* upon the party providing the indemnity. In either scenario, the party providing the indemnity will suffer a substantial loss. Depending upon the company and the ultimate extent of the loss, embarrassing explanations would need to be provided to shareholders, the stock exchange or even the financial press.

The insurance industry has undergone a massive change in the post–September 11th, 2001 and post–HIH/Enron/Arthur Andersen period.

There has been an exponential increase in insurance premiums to not only maintain the viability of the insurance industry, but also to deal with the increased risks that businesses now confront.

These changes affect every member of society as household, motoring and medical insurance premiums have dramatically increased. Indeed, with increasing regularity, insurers are even declining to insure what were once traditionally accepted risks.

With the increase in litigiousness in society, the situation may even deteriorate further. Corporations become the obvious target as they are increasingly perceived as having "deep pockets".

Insurance companies will increasingly require that corporations implement proactive risk management programmes and strategies with emphasis on the aim of preventing losses in the first place, as well as methods of minimising such losses once they occur.

■ ■ ■

Warranty and Indemnity (W&I) insurance

W&I insurance is often called Representations and Warranty (R&W) insurance in the USA.

In a transaction for the sale of shares in a company or the sale of a business, the buyer pays careful attention to the potential liabilities it may be taking on. Sale agreements often contain ceilings for liability beyond which the seller will not be liable (this is called a *liability cap*).

Parties to a transaction (along with their advisors) are *always* concerned about liability or loss arising out of warranties or indemnities relating to the transaction. It follows from this that they must also be concerned with the ability of the party giving such warranties and indemnities to be able to meet those obligations should they arise at some point in the future.

The key reason usually driving the decision to purchase this type of insurance cover is a concern about the financial ability of the seller to meet a warranty claim in the future. This can often arise where the selling company is either breaking up or at significant risk of falling into bankruptcy.

One other point to note: if the transaction is leveraged (that is, the purchaser is borrowing to finance the acquisition), it may be possible to obtain improved financing terms if the warranties are backed by an A rated insurance policy. The bank providing the acquisitions funds to the purchaser will be influenced by such a policy especially if there are concerns about the vendor's future financial position.

In the event that a buyer is concerned about the level of potential liabilities it will take on with the purchase, especially where the seller is reluctant to increase the liability cap (or otherwise accommodate the purchaser's concerns), a deadlock can often result.

During the course of a deal, these types of transactions tend to gather their own momentum. Often, if that momentum is lost, parties to the transaction can often lose the impetus to proceed with the deal.

One solution usually involves the retention of part of the sale proceeds. This is often referred to as holding monies *in trust* or *in escrow*. However this option often proves unattractive for the following reasons:

- it does not provide a "clean break" at the end of the transaction;

- the funds in escrow are not accessible;

- the real cost of the tied-up funds can be as much as 5% over a two year period;

- the time period of the escrow arrangement does not always equate with the time period of liability;

- access to the funds may only be ultimately available through litigation; and

- in the event of bankruptcy, access to the funds may be hindered.

However most sellers will want a "clean break". The reasons will vary:

- For example, where the seller is a private equity house (venture capitalist), it will need access to the entire sale proceeds for distribution to its investors.

- Where the seller is a privately owned (family) business, the owner may be retiring and does not wish to become involved in further dealings, after the finalisation of the sale transaction.

- Where the seller is a corporation, it may have a mandate from its parent to "cut the cord" or exit a business with no further involvement for strategic reasons (for example where the business no longer forms part of the parent organisation's "core business").

- That parties to a transaction wish to minimise the possibility of litigation occurring after completion of the sale.

Companies are becoming increasingly aware of the availability and convenience of the W&I insurance market, which has become significantly more active over the last few years. Often, parties will consider W&I insurance, not only for the convenience it offers, but with the aim of preserving the momentum of the negotiations of a deal. The purpose of such insurance is not to perfect a bad deal. If the deal is bad for a purchaser, a prudent underwriter is likely to also regard it as a bad one for the insurer.

For example, venture capitalists will rarely give warranties. This type of insurance can help plug such a hole in the deal. On occasions, a vendor unwilling to give warranties, in the ordinary course, could take out such cover (without the purchaser ever knowing this) and then proceed to give the necessary warranties. Otherwise, if the vendor were to have adhered to its stance of refusing to give warranties, the purchaser (assuming it even wished to proceed with the deal at all) would have required a massive reduction in the purchase price.

Where management are giving the warranties in the sale of a business and such management are to be retained by the purchaser to continue to run the business, it would neither be desirable nor feasible for a purchaser to sue its own management in the event of a breach of warranty. A preferable course is to have recourse to an appropriate policy of insurance.

■ ■ ■

To what agreements does W&I insurance apply?

W&I insurance applies to agreements effecting a change in the ownership of a business or company. Typically, this might take the form of the purchase and sale of:

• a business; or

• shares in a corporation.

There are two types of W&I insurance:

1) purchaser's W&I insurance — which generally covers a purchaser against its loss from a breach of a warranty by the vendor. Under this type of

policy, in order for the purchaser to have recourse to the policy, it must prove (to the insurer) that the vendor breached a warranty and demonstrate that such a breach caused the purchaser a quantifiable loss;

2) vendor's W&I insurance — which generally covers a vendor against liability in the event that it breaches a warranty given to the purchaser, as contained in the sale agreement. Under this type of policy, the purchaser needs to initiate legal action against the vendor and must prove (to the court) that the vendor breached a warranty and demonstrate that such a breach caused the purchaser a quantifiable loss. In the event of a successful court verdict against the vendor, the vendor can claim for reimbursement from the insurer under the policy.

■ ■ ■

What are the steps involved?

The largest international insurance brokers have specialists dealing in W&I insurance. Generally, one party's lawyer will approach a broker specialising in this form of insurance.

A usual first step is for the broker to obtain a lead underwriter's indication of the likely terms of the cover. This is done with a transaction summary and the second or third draft of the sale and purchase agreement. If the transaction is more complex, sufficient information will need to be provided to enable the insurer to gain an understanding of what the parties are seeking to achieve in the deal.

The broker will subsequently compare alternatives in the insurance market to secure the best solution in terms of price, extent of coverage tailored to the specific circumstances and structure of the transaction.

This process can generally be summarised as follows:

1) As with insurance generally, the broker collects the required information about the transaction. An insurer will usually require at least the following information to gain an understanding of the level of risk it is called upon to insure:

    ● a summary of the transaction, its value, the parties involved, the identity of their advisers (this aspect alone will cause the level of premium to fluctuate), and full details of which warranties and indemnities are to be insured;

- the full documentation of the transaction. This will be the sale and purchase agreement, where it is a standalone document. However, in more complex "big ticket" deals, the sale agreement will also be accompanied by collateral documents such as side letters and other documents containing warranties and indemnities. This will always include the warranty *disclosure letter* in the event that one exists;

- the full complement of financial statements of the corporation being sold; and

- any legal, accounting and taxation due diligence reports.

2) The broker will obtain quotations from insurers and select the most competitive in price and/or coverage as required.

3) The insurer will commission its own lawyers to carry out a limited *due diligence* which will include reviews of the warranties and indemnities and of all the documentation described above. The cost of such legal review is payable by the insured. In the event that the insurance cover is purchased, that cost is deducted from the premium assessed.

4) The parties to the insurance policy and to the sale and purchase agreement, through their lawyers and brokers, will negotiate the terms of the

insurance policy to ensure consistency with the sale documents.

5) A completed proposal form is then provided to the insurer.

6) Assuming all of the previous steps transpire satisfactorily, the insurance policy will then be executed and the premium must be paid.

From beginning to end, the process can take as little as under two weeks.

However, depending upon the complexity of the transaction, allowing at least three to four weeks would be more prudent. This will permit sufficient time to enable:

- the insurer's lawyers to complete their legal review of the documentation;

- the insurer's lawyers to obtain answers to any questions arising — or additional information or clarification required — during the process;

- the insurer to formally quote on the price and terms of the proposed cover, once the above steps are completed;

- sufficient time for any negotiations with the insurer, on the price and/or terms, to take place;

- the insurer to obtain the completed proposal form; and

- the insurer to finally incept (commence) the cover.

■ ■ ■

How much is the premium and how is it determined?

A once-only premium is payable upon entering into the insurance policy. This serves to overcome any concerns a buyer might have that a seller might fail to keep up premium payments and thereby cause the policy to lapse.

At the date of publication, the premiums for this type of coverage can range from about 3% and are usually somewhere between 4% and 8%, and sometimes as high as 10% of the limit of liability. In the future, one could expect these figures to rise.

In setting the premium the insurers take a number of factors into account:

- the level of complexity of the transaction;

- the limit of liability compared to the sale price;

- the scope of the cover agreed (for example, decreasing the excess or removing certain exclusions from the insurance policy, will tend to increase the premium);

- the financial stability of the parties;

- the type of business being sold;

- the amount of any *excess or deductible*;

- the identity of the professional advisers to the parties to the sale (where they are high calibre, the insurers have greater comfort that a thorough due diligence exercise will have been carried out and that, correspondingly, more liabilities will have been disclosed); and

- the nature of the warranties and indemnities. Generally, the more specific and highly defined they are, the lower the premium.

■ ■ ■

To what matters does the actual policy refer?

Each particular policy's terms and conditions will usually contain the following information:

- The name of the insured party;

- The company to be insured (the company being sold);

- Details of the insurer/s;

- Details of the parties to the sale agreement;

- The name of the party to whom any claim under the policy will be paid (that party is generally referred to by the insurer as the "loss payee"). For example, the Seller can take out the policy and name the Buyer as the loss payee;

- It will set out the precise warranties covered;

- It will define the specific breaches it will cover against;

- The nature of the losses covered;

- The amount of loss covered. Cover is limited to a specified amount (the limit of liability or limit of indemnity). It is a maximum aggregate limit (that is, any number of claims arising within the period of cover can be made up to this amount). Usually the limit is set at the amount of the consideration for the sale of the business or company, but this can vary (usually downwards);

- The amount of any excess or deductible. This is often tied to the *de minimis* warranty thresholds expressed in the sale and purchase agreement;

- The amount of premium;

- The duration of coverage. The term of the insurance cover usually runs concurrently with the duration of the underlying warranties and indemnities in the sale agreement (expressed as the time within which claims can be made). For non-tax warranties, this can usually last for two to three years , whereas, for tax warranties and indemnities, this can usually last for seven years;

- Any exclusions from coverage will be specifically defined (usually they will include such things as wilful acts, dishonesty, fraud, and environmental matters such as seepage and pollution).

The insurance policy will also contain terms relating to matters such as the claims notification procedures, conduct and settlement of claims for breach of warranty, governing law and assignment of contract.

■ ■ ■

Loss mitigation coverage

Loss mitigation coverage is available, providing insurance for known claims that may be uninsured or underinsured.

This could cover, for example, outstanding product liability or shareholder litigation claims, where the potential costs are a large variable.

Such a policy is not intended to cover known or foreseeable costs but to cover a "blow-out" of such costs. That is, where such costs turn out to be higher than originally anticipated.

Generally, the most common recurring areas arising in a sale of business transaction that most lend themselves to such a scenario are:

- litigation claims not covered by an insurance policy; and

- environmental liability such as that resulting from site contamination.

Given the unquantifiable nature of such potential exposures, any purchaser of a business carrying this kind of contingent liability is going to want to drive the price down by making a generous and prudent over-estimation of the contingency. All efforts will be made by a potential purchaser to over-estimate the contingency and avoid the necessity for future provisions and write-downs.

This type of cover enables (all or part of) the risk of a blow-out in costs to be transferred to an insurer.

An insurer will require quantification of the potential existing liability in order to provide cover beyond that amount. This effectively places a cap or ceiling on the maximum exposure. Both vendor and purchaser achieve certainty as to the maximum exposure.

Such cover can also offer protection against future changes to the law. For example, changes in environmental legislation might impact a corporation by substantially increasing its costs of decontaminating a site to even lower levels of contamination than previously ordered. An appropriate loss mitigation policy would effectively protect a corporation against such an (often unbudgeted) increase in costs.

Having this kind of cover in place enhances the vendor's leverage in negotiations to maximise the sale price, eliminating the need for an overly generous downward price adjustment to compensate for the purchaser's uncertainty.

Chapter 8

CONCLUSION

∎ ∎ ∎

We hope you will have gained an appreciation and understanding of the operation of indemnity clauses and the appropriate times and ways to use them.

By now you should also realise the great power that a carefully worded indemnity clause can wield and the potentially devastating effects it can have if not carefully scrutinised.

On the other hand, indemnity clauses, when used correctly, are great regulators of the apportionment of responsibility when things go wrong. In the correct context, they can be used to outsource liability where such liability is an inherent issue in the transaction.

Indemnity clauses, as with the rest of the contract documents themselves, are only ever consulted and relied upon when relationships between parties deteriorate to the extent that the "gloves come off". By then, the lines of communication have become severely strained or even severed.

Of course, the operation of logic and reason are not at their peak, by this stage of the game. Once the lawyers start advising the parties, it is generally in relation to the documents in isolation of the background and context of the dispute. Each party naturally presents a subjective view of the world to their lawyer. Naturally, lawyers are entitled to accept their clients' instructions as presented (save for any obviously blatant incongruities).

Even if you reach that stage, the knowledge in this book should adequately equip you to understand how the operation of an indemnity clause will apply to your particular case. You will also feel more confident in raising and discussing such issues with your lawyer, without feeling completely out of your depth.

Ideally, however, you will have gained an appreciation of how to evaluate an indemnity clause before accepting it in the first place. Now that you know what havoc an indemnity can wreak, you should not be embarrassed or think twice about referring a specific problem to your lawyer.

INDEX

Corporate Legal Education & Development (CLED) can assist your organisation

The author of this series, **Frank Adoranti**, is the principal of the specialised legal risk management consultancy *Corporate Legal Education & Development (CLED)*.

CLED is a specialist provider of legal risk management consultancy services to multinational corporations worldwide. Some of the range of services includes:

- legal audits (legal risk health checks);
- devising contract management solutions;
- other legal risk management advice;
- assistance in negotiating major contracts and deals;
- reviewing tenders and advising on major contract bids;
- specialised business consulting activities;
- formulating business and corporate policy;
- devising codes of conduct;
- crisis management planning and events;
- mergers and acquisitions;
- corporate restructuring;
- speaking at corporate functions and conventions;
- conducting training and seminars for management.

CLED provides such services in virtually any country in Asia, Europe or North America.

CLED is also able to assist you in working with the publisher for bulk and/or customised orders of the **Managers Guide Series** of books for your organisation.

To enquire about the possibility of having **Frank Adoranti** working with your organisation, please either:

- **fax** back this form to **+612 8824 9308**

or

- **email** your enquiry to: **frank@adoranti.com**

Name: ....

Organisation: ....

Country: ....

Title: ....

Email: ....

Tel: ....

Nature of enquiry: ....

....

....

Desired method of contact:

- Please phone me to discuss

- Please email me